JAPANESE PAINTING

JAPANESE PAINTING

A Brief History

by Kenji Toda

CHARLES E. TUTTLE COMPANY

RUTLAND, VERMONT & TOKYO, JAPAN

Representatives

For Continental Europe:
BOXER BOOKS INC. Zurich

For the British Isles:
PRENTICE-HALL INTERNATIONAL, INC. London

For Australasia:
PAUL FLESCH & CO., PTY. LTD. Melbourne

Published by the Charles E. Tuttle Company, Inc.
of Rutland, Vermont & Tokyo, Japan
with editorial offices at
Suido 1-chome, 2-6, Bunkyo-ku, Tokyo, Japan

Copyright in Japan, 1965 by
Charles E. Tuttle Co., Inc.

Library of Congress Catalog Card No. 65-22634

First printing, 1965

Book design and typography by John Paull

PRINTED IN JAPAN

Table of Contents

111 CHINESE SCHOOLS 53

❀ Introduction

This is a condensed graphic review of the history of Japanese painting from the seventh to the nineteenth centuries.

The illustrations have been selected to show the diversity of features in subject matter and the different forms of technique.

For some of the old paintings in damaged or faded condition, the author has made partly restored detail studies to bring out their basic organizations more clearly.

Additional information concerning these works and their historical backgrounds are given in the reference notes beginning on page 79.

Please note that all Japanese names mentioned in the text are according to Japanese custom; the family name first, followed by the given name.

The author's name is spelt in the Western manner.

1 ☯ Buddhist Schools

The introduction of Buddhism to Japan from China and Korea in the sixth and seventh centuries was accompanied with the introduction of an art that had been developing on the continent of Asia for centuries. Since the main purpose of this cultural impact was for Buddhist propagation, most of the art relics of this early period now extant in Japan are related to Buddhism. Some of them probably were brought from China or Korea. Some were made in Japan by the naturalized Chinese or Korean artists, or their descendants and Japanese associates. We have no exact knowledge about the artists who were responsible.

We can be sure, however, of the fact that these relics represent the standard of aesthetic appreciation cultivated in Japan of that time.

A tradition in taste and expression that developed out of religious inspiration can be traced through works of succeeding periods, even in the great variety of forms.

Japanese artists of the ninth and tenth centuries were no longer depending on Chinese models, and works such as Plates 6-8 demonstrate original expressions of monumental significance.

1. Tamamushi Portable Shrine

Total height 7 feet 8 inches, including base
Kept at Hōryūji Temple. No date of installation

Originally made for the household of Empress Suiko (553-628), the shrine is constructed of wood and covered with engraved bronze plates. Iridescent elytra of the Japanese beetle *yamato-tamamushi* (Chrysochroa fulgidissima) are mounted under the plates.

Pictures are painted on the doors and back of the shrine proper and on the four sides of the base.

2. Bosatsu on Shrine Doors

This work shows the characteristic form of female figures in Chinese art of the Six Dynasties (about A.D. 420-620). Bosatsu (Bodhisattva) are neuter but are generally represented in female costume.

A similar head covering with flying ribbons appears on a Lung-men cave sculpture of a goddess playing a zither.

Reference should also be made to the long narrow faces of ladies as represented in the famous Ku k'ai-chih scroll in the British Museum. These reflect the characteristic form of the Six Dynasties. Faces became rounder during the Tang period.

The pictures are faded, but the whole design can be clearly defined. Pictures on the Tamamushi Shrine are known as *mitsuda* painting. Pigments are mixed with a medium made of *mitsudasō* (a yellow powder derived by heating lead) and a vegetable-oil-like linseed. The painting has been applied on a black lacquer background.

3. Amida (Amita) of the Horyūji Frescoes
Detail shown about 4 feet high

Painted with two attending Bosatsu on the big wall (about 10 feet high and 8 ½ feet wide) on the west side of the Kondo hall of worship.

The temple was built in the seventh century, but the frescoes are considered to be a work of the early eighth century. The technique of shading in the delineation of the face and drapery is characteristic of Chinese painting of early T'ang period, when China had close communication with the Western world.

All paintings on the four big walls and eight small walls were damaged by fire in 1949, but many photographic reproductions were made prior to the disaster so that we have definite knowledge about the original condition. The fire destroyed all colors in the frescoes, but the contour lines remained intact on the plaster that withstood the heat. The pigments used in the frescoes were known to specialists making copies before the fire, so restoration was possible.

4. Bosatsu Seated on a Cloud

Kept at the treasure house Shōsōin

Ink drawing on cloth, 4 feet 5 inches square

Probably made as a base for embroidery. An interesting example of draughtmanship of an eighty-century artist. The spirited brushstrokes seem to show a natural skill resulting from long practice rather than a conscious display of technique. The same kind of draughtmanship is found in some of the masterpieces of *Yamato-e* scrolls of the twelfth century.

5. Kichijōten (Mahasri) of Yakushiji

Painted on cloth 18 inches high

This illustration is a partly restored detail of the standing image of the goddess.

A record of a special service held for Kichijōten at this temple in 773 suggests that the date of this work is in the late eighth century.

The full round face is typical of the T'ang women, in contrast to the narrow faces of the Six Dynasties. The general physiognomy, however, shows the beginning of more traces of a Japanese woman.

The technique of drapery shading, noticeable in the Hōryūji frescoes, is evident in this work.

6. Portrait of Gonzō Preaching
Attributed to Kūkai (774-835)
Detail from original kept at Fumon-in Monastery, Kōyasan
Painted on silk 4 ½ × 5 ½ feet

Priest Kūkai, known better as Kōbō Daishi, the founder of Kōyasan, received his first instruction in Buddhism from Gonzō (758-827). He was still under Gonzō's guidance when he entered Buddhist life in 793. Because of this relationship, the work was attributed to Kūkai.

Japanese scholars have never confirmed the exact date of this work, but the long inscription above this portrait points to an approximate period in 835-921.

In general style this work follows the form of T'ang Buddhist portraiture, but the individual characterization was evidently based on a life study. Together with the "Kichijōten" of Yakushiji, this portrait indicates a strong naturalistic school developing out of Japanese Buddhist painting of the eighth and ninth centuries.

7. Amida and His Hosts of Bosatsu *(above)*
Attributed to Eshin Sōzu (942-1017)
Centrepiece 7 feet square. Side pieces 3 ½ feet wide.
Kept at Koyasan Temple
Painted on silk.

The picture in triptych is a perfect example of fully developed Japanese Buddhist painting.

Seishi or Dai-Seishi (Mahasthamaprapta), representing the wisdom of Amida, is placed on his right, with Kannon or Kanzeon (Avalokitesvara), representing his mercy, left.

The conception of Amida's welcome to the Pure Land developed specifically in Japan, and there is no work comparable to the "Raigō" (Holy Welcome by Amida and his hosts) in China. For information see page 81.

8. Detail of Seishi Bosatsu in Plate 7 *(right)*
The expressions of Bosatsu in this painting of the late tenth or early eleventh century show Japanese characteristics.

11 ☯ Japanese Schools

The early history of the Japanese adaptation of continental civilization should be studied as a gradual process that started long before the introduction of Buddhism. All inhabitants of the island came from other lands originally, and some of them were probably aware at least of the existence of such forms of culture before they settled as a part of the Japanese people. Primitive art relics such as the potteries, clay figures, and some crude cave paintings that have been excavated in Kyushu since 1956 point to the different elements that characterize prehistoric Japanese culture. Blending of these various characters probably gave much flexibility to all cultural developments of the later periods.

The first Japanese painter of whom we have detailed historical records is Kudara no Kawanari (782-853). The name Kudara indicates that his family was of Korean extraction. Kawanari was a realistic painter of portraits and figure work. Kose no Kanaoka, known as the founder of the Japanese school, was active in about 859-900. Kose was one of the prominent families of the nation's leaders. According to old literary sources Kanaoka painted landscapes, animals, and Buddhist works. He is also recorded as a landscape architect. He worked for the imperial court and his descendants succeeded him as court painters.

As a branch of Kose in Buddhist painting, the line of Takuma developed in the late tenth century. Takuma painters in the later period adopted the form of Chinese Buddhist works of the Sung period.

The school of Tosa, which is generally recognized as the main line of *Yamato-e,* the Japanese painting, originated with a group of Buddhist painters of the Fujiwara family called Kasuga. This name was adopted because they worked for the Kasuga shrine in Nara. Kasuga is a Shinto shrine but the strong influence of Buddhism made the Shinto priests incorporate the Buddhist element into their creed. Both Kasuga, the tutelary deity, and Kкfukuji temple had a special relation with the powerful Fujiwara clan.

A branch of Tosa called Sumiyoshi was established in 1662 to perpetuate the line of Sumiyoshi Keion, a great master of the early thirteenth century. A famous scroll painting by Keion is kept at the Boston Museum of Fine Arts. Keion left no successors and it was decided to appoint an able painter, Tosa Hiromichi (1559-1670), as heir with the name Sumiyoshi Jokei. His son Gukei (1631-1705) became an official painter to Tokugawa. No marked technical characteristics distinguish the works of these branches of the Japanese school, and the term Yamato-e can be used to include them all.

Japanese painters were able to express themselves freely with any local subject in nature as well as intimate humanity by the ninth and tenth centuries. *(Toda, Japanese Screen Paintings of the Ninth and Tenth Centuries. Ars Orientalis, Vol. III. 1959.)* Yamato-e reached its peak of development in the twelfth century. Buddhist paintings were preserved

24

in the sanctuary of temples, but most of the works in large scale, painted on screens and sliding doors of palaces and mansions, perished with the buildings when ravaged by fire. Small hand scrolls and albums were comparatively safe as they could be easily stored or carried to safety. There are now about one hundred of these works extant in Japan, and they give us valuable material to trace the development of Japanese painting. These small pictures were not made by miniature specialists but by artists who were trained to paint larger pictures, and the freedom and power of their art show even in small scale.

A strong tendency to select decorative elements in nature is a leading characteristic of Japanese painting. Such tendency is evident in the works of the twelfth century (Plates 11 & 16). Two masters of the decorative school, Honnami Kōetsu (1557-1637) and Tawaraya Sōtatsu (?-1643), based their works on those old Yamato-e. Ogata Kōrin (1655-1716) and his brother Kenzan (1664-1743) were the followers of Kōetsu and Sōtatsu.

The school of popular genre, *ukiyo-e,* is represented mainly by the wood block prints of the period from late seventeenth to nineteenth century. The development of ukiyo-e, however, should be traced back to the early seventeenth century when many superb genre were painted by unknown masters. The first introduction of Western culture to Japan by the Jesuit missionaries in the sixteenth century probably was partly responsible as a new stimulant for this development. *Toda, The Effect of the First Great Impact of Western Culture in Japan. Journal of World History, Vol. II, No. 2, UNESCO 1954.*

9. Nachi Waterfall
Attributed to Kose no Kanaoka
Kept in the Nezu Collection
Painted on silk 23 × 63 inches

Many features distinguish this work as a rare example of the early form of Japanese landscape painting. The technique is similar to the garment delineation in the Gonzō portrait (See Plate 6). Elaborate shading in ink wash and color is used for the ground work, with only traces of line. (Compare Plate 17 with predominant contour lines.)

A poem composed about a screen painting of a waterfall in the palace of Emperor Montoku (827-858), included in the collection of Kokin-shū (compiled in 905), suggests that the painting of such landscapes were not uncommon in the ninth century.

10. Beckoning at the Moon

Attributed to Fujiwara no Tadayoshi,
Kept at the Tokugawa Collection, Nagoya
Painted on paper measuring 8 ¾ inches vertically

This hand scroll of the early twelfth century represents scenes from the "Tales of Genji." This scene is from Chapter 45 of "Genji Monogatari," showing the princess beckoning at the moon with her lute plectrum.

The tendency to organize masses into decorative design is evident in this form of painting.

11. New Year on a Kyoto Boulevard *(left)*
Attributed to Fujiwara no Mitsunaga

Crowds of people line an avenue to watch the imperial procession and experience the excitements of the day. The vigorous action of men and animals is in strong contrast to the static arrangements of plum trees, shown overleaf.

All important features of the Japanese School can be found in this monumental work, that is, the expression of movement in organization.

Detail below expresses movement vividly.

12. New Year at the Palace *(above)*
Attributed to Fujiwara no Mitsunaga
Painted on paper measuring 19 inches vertically

This picture and those shown in Plate 11 are from Roll 1 of the hand scroll "Nenjū Gyōji" (Rites and Festivities of the New Year). These pictures represent scenes on the 2nd day of New Year when the emperor would make a formal call to the palace of his parents.

Details at left show decorative plum trees.

(See Reference Notes for information on this work.)

13. Two Types of Action Drawing

Fighting Cocks *(above)* from Roll 15 of "Nenjū Gyōji" by Mitsunaga. Parties for cock fights were given in the 3rd month, and the scroll shows scenes of aristocrats in a garden, and country folk in the yard of a small shrine.

Game of *gitchō (left)* is from the scroll of cartoons of men and animals attributed to Toba Sōjō, kept at the Tokyo Museum. Ink on paper measuring vertically 12 ¼ inches. A similar scene is given in the scroll by Mitsunaga. Costumes of the players in both cases show that the game was played by the common people.

14. Hospitality for the Unusual Traveler

Attributed to Sojo (1053-1140)
Kept at Nara Museum
Painted on paper measuring 12 ½ inches vertically

From Roll 3 of the hand scroll "Shigisan Engi." One of
the finest examples of narrative painting. This scene shows

an old nun pausing on her journey to Nara. She has come from Shinano province to find her young brother who had left home years ago to study Buddhism in the capital.

As the horse is being unsaddled, the nun removes her riding boots. Attendants are bringing a lamp and refreshments, and an old couple at right foreground select fruit.

15. Kichijoten of Joruriji

Statue, 35 ½ inches high

Famous as the finest Japanese polychrome wooden sculpture of the late eleventh or early twelfth century. The simple design of its shrine and the elaborate Buddhist figures painted inside are worth special studies. Our present interest, however, concerns the picture decorating the outside of the front doors. *(facing page)*

16. Bamboo and Sparrows *(below)*

Each door measures 12 ½ × 41 ½ inches

Done on wood with heavy paints, the main stem is split in the centre, with right and left halves forming the front edges of the doors. When the doors are closed, the split halves join together to form a complete stem, with branches spreading out on both sides, forming a decorative tree.

17. The Cascade *(detail)*
Artist unknown
Kept at Chion-in Temple, Kyoto
Painted on silk 57 × 61 inches
The complete painting depicts a typical Japanese landscape. The strong contour lines defining the ground formations represent the characteristic Chinese influence of the thirteenth century. The centre of this work (not shown) is occupied by Amida and the heavenly host.

18. Hills in Snow

By En-i

Kept at Kyōto Museum

Painted on silk measuring vertically 15 inches

A scene from Roll 5 of the hand scroll representing the life of priest Ippen Shōnin (1239-1289) and dated Shōan 1 (1299). Ippen was a traveling evangelist, and the scenes of his preaching in various provinces present a good series of landscape painting. Very little is known about the artist En-i. The name suggests that he was probably a Buddhist painter. No other work by this artist has been discovered.

19. Seascape on Sliding Doors
By Takashima Takakane
Twenty rolls on silk measuring vertically 16 ¼ inches
Scene from Roll 3 of the hand scroll "Kasuga Gongen Kenki" and dated Enkei 2 (1309).

Noted not only as a masterpiece in *Yamato-e,* but also as a valuable source for antiquarian studies because of the accurate drawings. A similar composition of rocks and pine trees on sliding doors is found in Chapter 36 of the "Genji Monogatari" scroll by Takayoshi.

Since no extant sliding doors with paintings of those daysare available, these hand scroll illustrations are valuable reference, and give us some idea of the subjects chosen for interior decoration.

20. White Rabbit and Lespedeza Flowers
By Honnami Kōetsu (1557-1637)

The classical poem, written in the artist's own calligraphy, expresses the following sentiment:

"I wish a person would have the heart
to inquire even incidentally,
For whose sake I have the moonlight
dwell upon my sleeves."

This poem is a favorite subject in Japanese painting. The flower blooms in autumn; the rabbit suggests the moon. Thus the poem gives the sentiment of an autumn evening.

21. Iris along the Foot-bridge *(right)*
By Ogata Kōrin (1655-1716)

Cover of an ink-stone-and-brush case, painted in lacquer. Leaves are gold; flowers are inlaid mother-of-pearl; and the bridge is inlaid pieces of lead.

22. Dancing Women

Artist unknown. Early seventeenth century.

Part of a pair of *kakemono* representing a group of men and women dancing outdoors. Many interesting pictures of the life of people painted in the late sixteenth and early seventeenth centuries are anonymous. Some are considered to be of the Kano school. The form of painting, in the majority of cases, belong decidedly to the Japanese school.

23. Night Rain at Karasaki *(below)*
By Andō Hiroshige (1797-1858) Color print, 10× 15 inches,
Courtesy of the Art Institute of Chicago
From the series "Eight Views around Lake Biwa."
    Hiroshige unquestionably is one of the representatives
of Japanese landscape painters. His contribution to the
history of Japanese painting, however, is more as a print
designer than as a painter. The printing process gives special
effects which are difficult to reproduce by painting.

48 PART TWO

24. Autumn Evening at a Green House
By Torii Kiyonaga (1752–1815) Color print, 10 × 15 inches
Courtesy of the Art Institute of Chicago

From the series "Twelve Months of the South."

In the masterpieces of *ukiyo-e* prints of beautiful women by such artists as Suzuki Harunobu (1725–1770), Kitagawa Utamaro (1753–1806), or Kiyonaga, one is impressed by a certain dignity even in the representation of prostitutes.

25. Warrior and Horse Swimming a Rapid
After Katsushika Hokusai (1760–1849)

Book illustration for *Ehon Musashi Abumi,* published in 1836. The original picture is cut into two halves for the convenience of publication.

Hokusai developed a special form in the field of warrior

pictures. In a note given on this work, he expresses his opinion that an effective painting of force in action should be bold and direct, and fanciful techniques should be avoided. The artist's interest in studies of horses and military art is noted in Vol. 6 of the *Manga*.

111 ✷ Chinese Schools and the Eclectics

Japanese painting developed as a branch of Chinese painting. Materials such as brush, ink, colors, paper and silk, together with the forms of representation of objects, were all of Chinese origin. The influence of Chinese Buddhist works in the early period has been reviewed previously in Part I. In the tenth and eleventh centuries when Japan's own cultural ground was firmly established, Chinese paintings, called *Kara-e* to distinguish them from the Japanese painting *Yamato-e,* were still appreciated for their exotic features. But we find no record about the artists who specified in *Kara-e.* Japanese painters in those days probably did not specialize much in their styles. The real specialists in Chinese schools are found after the fourteenth century.

Since the first introduction of the Zen sect of Buddhism by the priest Eisai (1140-1215) who made two trips to China in the latter part of the twelfth century, many Japanese priests went to China to study Zen and a number of eminent Chinese priests were invited to come to Japan. Two famous Zen temples in Kamakura, Kenchōji and Enkakuji, were built in the thirteenth century with Chinese priests as their founders. A form of ink painting which developed in China during the Sung period (960-1279), was introduced to Japan by some of these Zen priests.

The first Japanese artist who specialized in Chinese painting is the priest Kaō (?-1345) of Nanzenji in Kyoto. This priest went to China in 1317 and stayed there for about ten years. In the early fifteenth century two priests in Kyoto, Minchō (1352-1431) of Tōfukuji and Shūbun of Shōkokuji, were distinguished painters of the Sung schools, the former in Buddhist and the latter in landscape works. The famous masters Sesshū (1420-1506) and Kano Masanobu (1453-1490) received their early training in painting under Shūbun. Sesshū was a Zen priest but Masanobu was a professional artist in service of the *shōgun* Ashikaga Yoshimasa. Masanobu founded the Kano school. Kano painters succeeded in combining a variety of techniques in Chinese and Japanese schools. Their efficiency and broad scope made them the official painters for the Tokugawa regime. With hundreds of followers all over the country they held great influence in various fields of Japanese painting from the seventeenth to early nineteenth century.

Both Sesshū and Kano modeled their works after what Chinese art critics called the Northern school, which was essentially a part of the great development of landscape paintng in the Sung period. The works of Northern the school are characterized by masterful draftsmanship and highly dolished brush technique. There were, however, a number of Sung landscape painters who aimed more at the expression of their own moods in their own direct contact with nature, than at mere technical display. Their attitude appealed to the intellectuals, and many scholars and poets began to make their own attempts in painting. This movement contiinued through the Yuan (1280-1368),

Ming (1368-1644), and the Ch'ing (1662-1911) periods.

The first definition of Northern and Southern schools is found in the book *Hua-ch'an-shih Sui-pi (Notes from the Zen Studio of Painting)* by Tung Ch'i-chang (1555-1636), a scholar, painter, and calligraphist who advocated the Southern school as the art of literati.

The first introduction of this Southern literati school to Japan was made again by Chinese priests of the Zen sect. In the mid-seventeenth century the Ming dynasty was in decline, and a number of Chinese intellectuals sought refuge in Japan from the political troubles at home. Among them were Zen priests who were painters of the literati school. Their works revealed a new field in expression and attracted many Japanese followers.

Meanwhile, Chinese publications on painting were introduced and some able Chinese painters came to Nagasaki to find markets for their works and to give instruction. The study of Chinese classics was encouraged by the Tokugawa government, and the new Chinese influence persisted until the great impact of Western culture swept the country in the latter part of the last century.

Besides the more abstract literati works, a Chinese form of detailed naturalistic painting of flowers and birds was introduced in the early eighteenth century. These new revelations led many Japanese painters to study actual works and reproductions of Chinese paintings which were brought to Japan since the time of the Ashikaga *shıgun* and kept in temples and private collections. Thus resulted the great variety of eclectic works that have continued until the present in Japan.

26. Kanzan (Han-shan)
By Kaō (?-1345)
Ink on paper 13 ¼ × 39 inches

This work shows that the artist was in full control of Chinese technique. According to Zen legends, Kanzan and his friend Juttoku (Shih-te) were associated in the early T'ang period with the Zen master Bukan (Feng-kan) from the temple Kuo-ch'ing-ssu of T'ien-t'ai-shan.

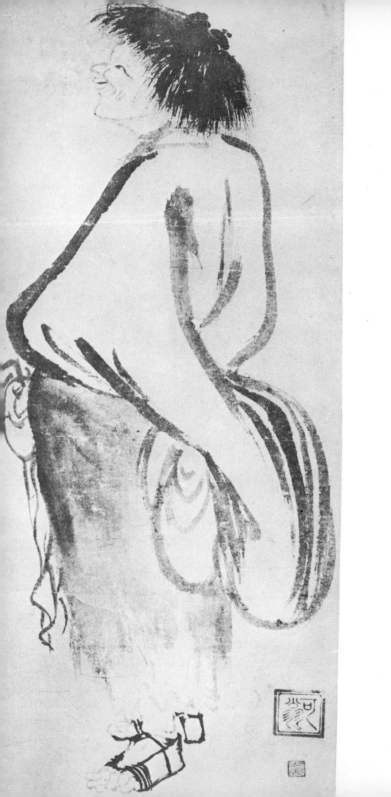

27. Chinese Landscape
By Shūbun
Ink on paper 13 × 42 ¾ inches

Exact dates on the life of Shūbun are not clear. It is re-corded that he received instruction in painting from Josetsu, another priest at Shōkokuji, who was probably a pupil of a Chinese Zen priest.

Plates 26-30, 34-35 show only a few examples of the infinite technical variations in the use of brush and ink.

28. Landscape
By Shukō (1412-1502)
Ink on paper 8 ¾ × 17 ¾ inches

Shukō was a Zen priest at Daitokuji and received instruction in painting from Nō-ami (1397-1476), a pupil of Shūbun whose works tended more to the Southern school. Shukō developed a form of serving tea which attracted the attention of the shogun Ashikaga Yoshimasa who made him leave the temple and join the artists in his service. In this respect Shukō is considered the founder of Japanese tea ceremony. His technique seems to suggest the simple dignity of the "Tea."

29. Chinese Landscape
By Sesshū (1420-1506)
Kept at Tokyo Museum
Ink on paper 11 ½ × 18 ¾ inches

This picture, "Summer," is one of a famous pair. The other, "Winter," is painted on the same scale. Sesshū's technique is close to that of the Sung master Hsia Kuei.

30. Rain

By Shūgetsu

Ink or paper 9 × 18 ½ inches

This artist, formerly a samurai in the service of Lord Shima-
zu in Kyūshū, became a Buddhist priest and accompanied
his master Sesshū on a trip to China in 1468. He was more
than seventy years old when he died in Kyūshū during the
Eisho era (1504-1520). The "Ink Splash" was this artist's
favorite technique.

31. Cherry Tree in Full Bloom *(overleaf)*
Attributed to Kano Sanraku (1559-1635)
Kept at the monastery Chishaku-in, Kyōto
Painted originally for sliding doors, but mounted later as a wall painting in four sections. The blossoms are modeled in relief in heavy white paint on a gold background.

Sanraku was a pupil and adopted son of Kano Eitoku (1543-1590) but developed his own style by combining naturalistic studies with the decorative elements of the old *Yamato-e* and Chinese structural brush technique.

32. Portrait of Kaihoku Yusho and His Wife *(right)*
By their son, Kaihoku Yūsetsu (1598-1677)
The artist Yūsetsu received his early training under his father, a pupil of Eitoku, whose characteristic style differs somewhat from regular Kano. Yūsetsu followed after Kano form and was an official painter for Tokugawa.
(For information about this portrait see p. 93.)

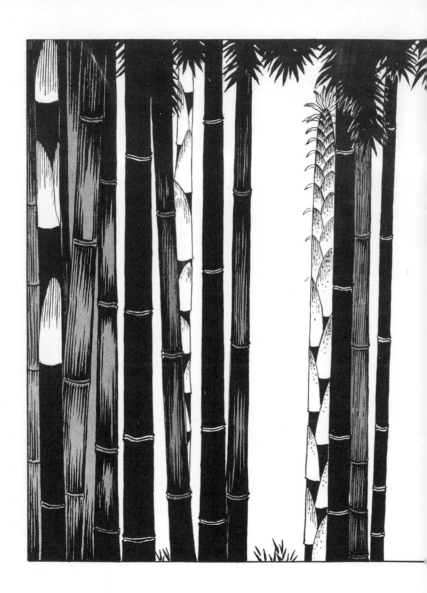

70   PART THREE

33. Bamboo Groove *(overleaf)*
Attributed to Kano Sanraku (1559-1635)
Kept at Tenkyu-in monastery Kyōto
Painted on paper in ink and heavy green paint.

Eitoku, Sanraku, Kaihoku Yūshō (1533-1615), and Hasegawa Tōhaku (1539-1610) are known as the masters of the Momoyama paintings. Their works on screens and sliding doors were made mainly for the decoration of Momoyama (Peach Hill) Castle, Fushimi, near Kyoto, the residence of Japan's Napoleon, Toyotomi Hideyoshi (1537-1598).

34. Pine Tree *(right)*
Maruyama Okyo (1733-95)
Painted on silk 22 × 51 inches

Ōkyo took his name after Sen Shunkyō (Chien Shun-chu), the specialist in flowers and birds of the early Uuan period.

The dexterity of Ōkyo's art seems to have its source in Chinese painting, but he was able to use that skill for his own naturalistic studies. This dexterity in the use of brush and ink is characteristic of the Maruyama and Shijō schools which were developed by the followers of Ōkyo in Kyoto.

35. Bamboos
By Gion Nankai (1677-1751)
By Gion Nankai (1677-1751) and Ikeno Taigadō (1723-76)
Ink on paper

Nankai was a scholar in Chinese classics serving the lord of Wakayama. He was a highly talented person who distinguished himself with poetry in Chinese form when he was fourteen and was self-taught as a painter.

Taigadō made a special trip to Wakayama to ask Nankai for instruction in painting, and it was Nankai's advice that made Taigadō find his own course of study in painting. Nankai and Taigadō are representative followers of the Chinese literati school (Southern Sung) in Japan.

36. Peacock
By Okamoto Shūki (1785-1862)
Painted on silk

Shūki was a pupil of Watanabe Kazan (1793-1841), the noted painter of the Chinese Southern school. Shūki, however, based his work upon his own study of nature, establishing a distinguished form in painting flowers and birds. Delineation of minute details, without losing the lifelike expression of the bird, shows characteristics more akin to Chinese paintings of flowers, birds, and insects.

◉ Reference Notes

Plate 1

(1) According to the latest studies by Japanese specialists in entomology, the elytra used on the Tamamushi Shrine are of a strictly Japanese type of beetle. This fact seems to prove that the shrine was made in Japan, even if Chinese artists were employed for the work. We understand that the elytra character of Chinese or Korean species of *chryso-chroa* can be distinguished very readily from that of the Japanese species *fulgidissima*. Examples of *tamamushi* elytra for the decoration of arrow shafts and knife handles are found among the treasures of Shōsōin.

(2) Together with the Tamamushi Shrine, another portable shrine called the Shrine of Lady Tachibana is kept at Hōryūji. This shrine is somewhat simpler in construction, with a total height of about 9 feet. Geometrical decorative designs are painted on the broad flat roof of the shrine proper. Four walls of the stand have paintings on a white background without lacquer. On the two front doors of the shrine, four standings figures of Bosatus are painted in gold line on a black lacquer background. The style of painting on this shrine is that of the early T'ang period, in contrast to that of the Six Dyansties in the paintings of Tamamushi Shrine.

Plate 5

(1) A work that shows close resemblance to this painting of Kichijōten is the six-panel screen "Ladies Under Trees" kept at Shōsōin. This screen was decorated with feathers on the head and garments originally, but the feathers have come off and only the basic contour lines can be seen in its present condition. The physiognomies of these ladies are similar to the goddess; the only difference lies in the use of rouge on the cheeks, a characteristic of Chinese painting which evidently was not to Japanese taste, as rouge on cheeks is rarely found in Japanese paintings of women. This screen was given to the temple Tōdaiji by the Empress in 757, in memory of Emperor Shōmu.

(2) The last volume (Vol. XX) of *Manyō-shū* contains many poems by young men who were drafted and sent to Kyūshū for defense service. In a group of seven poems, dated Tenpyō-shōhō 7 (A.D. 755), we find the following:

"*Waga tsuma mo*

my wife

e ni kaki toran

I would like to have painted

izuma mo ga

for while being apart traveling,

tabi yuku ware wa

I shall keep her close to my heart

mitsutsu shinuban

by looking at it."

This poem seems to suggest that portrait painting was common among Japanese people of the eighth century even though works like the picture of Kichijōten were not for general use.

80 REFERENCE NOTES

(3) The portrait of Prince Shōtoku with his two sons, kept in the Imperial Collection, is known as the oldest portrait painting in Japan. This work, attributed to a Korean prince who visited Japan in A.D. 597, is painted on soft-surface paper without sizing. The technique consists of line drawing with color and light shading. Heavy ink on the eyebrows and deep vermilion on the lips show features similar to the painting of Kichijōten. It was probably a fashion in the Far East in those days to have eyebrows and lips vividly shown in a portrait. Shading is done in grazed ink strokes, as an ink wash would not work well on un-sized paper.

The standing figure of Prince Shōtoku in the center is about 2 feet in height. The artist's effort to give individual character to the physiognomy of the three faces is evident.

Plate 7

Priest Genshin (942-1017) was called Eshin Sōzu, the abbot of Eshin, because he lived at the monastery Eshin-in of Hieizan. He commenced Buddhist life in his youth and studied under Priest Ryōgen (913-987), the bishop of Enryakuji. Ryōgen founded the monastery Eshin-in at Yokawa on Mt. Hiei, more than two miles from the main temple buildings at Enryakuji. Genshin retired to this quiet monastery around 970 to devote himself seriously to the study of Buddhism. Fifteen works on Buddhist doctrines are credited to him, and correspondence with the Chinese priest Chih-li in 1003 is recorded in the Sung publication *Ssu-ming Chiao-ming-lu*. Besides his scholarly accomplishments, Genshin is remembered for his popular work *Ojō Yōshū*. This book is in three parts, the first two parts giving a description of a sinful world and the horrors of hell and the last part describing the eternal happiness of the Pure Land of Amida. The welcome of the holy hosts, *Shōju Raigō,* is described in Chapter I of the third part.

More than twenty paintings are attributed to Eshin Sōzu, most of them showing Amida and attending Bosatsu. The biography of Genshin Sōzu, kept at Shuryōgon monastery of Yokawa on Hieizan, mentions that he painted "Amida Raigō" after his own study of the sutra. The book *Go-Shūi-ōjō-den* by Miyoshi Tameyasu (1049-1139), a court mathematician who was interested in the biographies of noted priests, gives an account of Eshin's painting of the "Heavenly Welcome," made especially for the famous general, Taira no Koremochi.

The painting of "Raigō" at Kōyasan bears a note mounted on its back dated Tenshō 15 (1537). We learn from the note that this work was originally kept at Hieizan and was known to be Eshin's, painted when he was 24 years old. This note indicates that the picture was in poor condition, and much effort was made to remount it for preservation. The picture, originally painted in one piece, was then made into the present triptych. Two later repairs are recorded, one in 1778, and the other in 1908.

There seems to be no question about Eshin's activities as a painter, but it does not seem possible that a 24 year old priest who had been devoting his time to scholarly works could master to such a high degree, technique in painting as we find in the work at Kōyasan. There is, however, a painting of Shōju Raigō kept at the temple Saikyōji of Sakamoto at the foot of Hieizan that bears a note in Eshin's own writing. This note states that in the 12th month of

Shōreki 5 (994), Genshin, priest of the Tendai sect, reverently painted this picture showing Amida's gracious guiding influence. It seems more likely that after the age of fifty, he had more time to cultivate his ability as an artist. We may assume that he was interested in painting and that he originated the conception of Raigō even though he first asked professionals to paint the pictures for him.

We give a place of special importance to Eshin Sōzu in our study of the history of Japanese painting because of his introduction of the subject of Raigō. Eshin was a priest of the Tendai sect and did not found a new sect, but his *Ojō Yōshū* inspired the priest Hōnen (1132-1211) who founded the Jōdo sect. Hōnen was followed by Shinran (1173-1262), the founder of Jōdo Shinshū. Emphasis on the simple faith of complete dependence on the grace of Amida made the religion readily understandable to all classes of people, and the two sects still have the greatest number of followers among sects in present day Japan.

The effect of the faith of Jōdo (Pure Land) in the field of painting is twofold. It produced the Raigō and helped introduce the subject of landscape into Buddhist painting. Consequently these two features bestow the rich elements of humanity that distinguish Japanese Buddhist art from the art of other countries with Buddhist faith.

Works like the Raigō of Kōyasan and Chion-in can represent Japan among the masterpieces of the world's religious paintings.

The conception of the joyous heavenly hosts coming down to receive the believer's soul is strictly Japanese. The use of the two Chinese characters *rai* (come) and *gei* (receive)—pronounced gō in this particular term, with special significance—seems to have originated in Japan. This compound is not given in the Chinese dictionaries since its use found in the texts of some sutras has no other meaning than a mere verb. No mention is made of the picture of Raigō in the two standard classics of the history of Chinese painting. In Vol. III of *Li-tai Ming-hua Chi (Record of Famous Paintings of the Successive Dynasties),* written by Chang Yen-yuan in A.D. 847, we find a list of over 160 Buddhist wall paintings then extant in China.

In 845, the emperor Wu-tsung, an ardent follower of Taoism, destroyed 4600 Buddhist temples and forced 26,000 priests and nuns to abandon their faith. Thus some Buddhist works, as Chang Yen-yuan carefully noted, were then moved to private collections for preservation. At any rate, Raigō is not included in the list. In Vols. I-IV of *Hsuan-ho Hua-pu,* record of the imperial collection of the Sung period, compiled in A.D. 1120, we find impressive lists of over 1,000 Buddhist and Taoist paintings from the Six Dynasties to Sung. Here again we fail to find even a single recorded example of a picture of Raigō.

A number of landscape paintings on the temple walls are recorded in the list of Chang Yen-yuan, but they seem to indicate either some works of Taoist influence or pictures of decorative purpose. The representation of Amida with Kannon and Seishi appearing over the hills is popularly considered to have its origin in the inspiration of Eshin Sōzu. The introduction of landscape to Buddhist painting is characteristic of the Jōdo sect which emphasizes close relation of Amida to man's life. This beautiful scene can be conceived as the realization of Pure Land on earth.

For a good example of landscape in Japanese Buddhist

painting, mention must be made of the wall painting of the Phoenix Shrine at the temple Byōdō-in in Uji. This hall, built in 1053 and containing a wooden statue of Amida, is well preserved, but the paintings on the walls and doors are not in good condition. However, the main feature, representing typical Japanese landscape like that we find in the Raigō at Chion-in, can be traced without difficulty.

Plates 10, 11, 12, 13

For almost four hundred years—from the transfer of the capital from Nara to Kyoto in 794 to the establishment of military government at Kamakura in 1192—the imperial court retained the actual power as the center of administration. Since the aristocrats of the Fujiwara clan were the most influential at the court, Japanese culture during this period is usually called the culture of the aristocrats. It has often been argued that the artists were supported by the aristocrats and worked only for the demands of aristocratic people in their life of luxury and pleasure.

This argument is based on two assumptions: that the interest of court people was confined only to their own surroundings, and that the artists worked only for the interest of their patrons. We have no place in this study to present many examples of art and literary sources to discuss this argument, but the hand scroll of "Nenjū Gyōji" is selected as material that may help us to survey this matter.

This hand scroll, originally made in sixty rolls and kept at the imperial court, unquestionably was painted for the demands of the emperor and court people. There are many dated records about painting the chief events of the year on screens of the tenth century, and we can assume that interest in such pictures was common to aristocratic circles.

The importance of this work was recognized by connoisseurs in later periods, and a number of copies were made. In 1626 a copy of about twenty rolls was made by Sumiyoshi Jokei, his son Gukei, and their assistants, under imperial order. The original sixty rolls were destroyed by fire at the palace in 1653. Evidently some other copies were made previously for some daimyo, for we find copies made by the Kano artists in 1774-1823 based chiefly upon copies in the collection of Matsudaira Sadanobu (1758-1829), the lord of Shirakawa who was noted as an able statesman and patron of art.

The copy made by the Sumiyoshi artists is in the collection of Mr. Shinbi Tanaka, the well known authority on Japanese painting, whose family is related to Sumiyoshi. The copy made by Kano artists is kept at the Tokyo Museum. By comparing these two copies one may judge how faithful they are to the original. The present writer had an opportunity to study the whole work at the Tokyo Museum. He also has in his possession a photographic reproduction of the 19 rolls of Sumiyoshi copy, published in 1931 by Yūzankaku of Tokyo.

The attribution of the original to Mitsunaga of the twelfth century lacks conclusive evidence. Our primary interest is in the quality of the work and the fact that it was kept at the imperial palace, indicating that the artist or artists who painted them worked for the aristocrats. As to the quality of the work, the masterful draftsmanship is manifest even in the copies. We do not find such force of expression and technical versatility in the dated or signed works of the later periods after the thirteenth century when the Japanese school was beginning to formalize.

The monumental scale, at least in volume, of this work gives us a comprehensive view of (a) the subjects in which the aristocrats were interested and (b) the art that expressed their interests. We have no space in this condensed study to give a detailed description of the entire work. A few of them may be sufficient for general information.

The average size of the rolls vertically is about 19 inches, and they unroll horizontally to a length of from 10 to 30 feet. According to the scheme of painting on hand scrolls, pictures are painted in continuity throughout the whole length, but the boundary of each scene can be readily distinguished. In Roll 1, there are four scenes: (1) the emperor about to leave his palace for a New Year call on his parents (2) outside the palace gates (3) along the route of the imperial procession (4) at the palace of the ex-emperor.

The individual characterization and movement of hundreds of people and animals in these scenes show the keen power of observation and consummate ability of the artist. The tendency to organize plant forms into decorative patterns can also be observed. Roll 1 represents the life of the aristocrats, although groups of common people are introduced in Scene 3.

With the festival of Kamo Shrine in the fourth month as the center of interest, Rolls 4 and 5 are almost entirely devoted to the life of common people. We find the festival parade; boys in a war game are joined by men probably under the influence of sake. In Roll 6 *dengaku* dancers perform in the street, and in Roll 15, a rural scene of a cock-fight, we find no indication of the luxury of court people. One may explain the interest of the aristocrats in such scenes as mere curiosity, but one should remember that an artist cannot paint a good picture without interest and sympathy in the subject.

The technique of the Japanese school undoubtedly originated in Buddhist painting. Japanese painters of the ninth and tenth centuries, however, were already beginning to express their interest in local subjects, outside of the religious pictures which still constituted the chief source of their subject matter. With their art thus developed, the artists found joy in expressing their own interests with fresh and vivid images drawn from their environment.

The vitality of Japanese painting reached its peak in the twelfth century, and the two names Mitsunaga and Toba Sōjō represent artists who represented the standard established in that period. The grand architectural composition of the palace buildings with the groups of court nobles in Roll 9 show the ability of an artist who was trained to paint large scale pictures on screens or sliding doors. On the same roll, a scene showing six court ladies dancing on a specially prepared stage is a rare example of twelfth-century subjects in genuine costume.

In a survey of Japanese painting of the twelfth century, the hand scroll attributed to Takayoshi (Plate 10) is usually taken as typical art of the aristocrats. The organization of pictures into color patterns, in contrast to the strong expressive brush strokes one finds in the works by the artists like Mitsunaga or Toba Sōjō, seems to represent the luxury of court life very effectively. Some students see two lines of development: the color work exclusively from the court and work with expressive brush strokes from the temples.

In the esoteric system of the Shingon sect, priests copied hundreds of Buddhist images so they could cultivate their memories and thus identify each character readily. A valuable collection of such drawings is kept at the temple Daigoji in Kyoto. A clean-cut distinction between the court and temple artists, however, may not explain the actual situation. The "Nenjū Gyōji" scroll was made at the court, but the work is full of expressive brush strokes.

Paintings with predominant designs in color and figures with simplified facial features are found in many works of approximately the same period. The famous thirty-three rolls of illuminated sutra (dated 1164) kept at Itsukushima shrine and the two works of Nezame Monogatari and Murasaki Shikibu Nikki, both attributed to Fujiwara no Nobuzane (1177-1265), definitely represent court life. But in a group of paintings done on over 100 sheets of fan-shaped paper kept at the temple Shitennōji in Osaka are many intimate scenes of the life of common people. *(Toda, The Shitennōji Albums of Painted Fans, Ars Orientalis, Vol. 4, 1961.)* The form of painting in this work is similar to the Itsukushima scroll, and there is no doubt that they were made for the aristocrats, as only persons of wealth could afford such works.

Plate 18

Priest Ippen (1239-1289) entered the Buddhist life when he was fifteen years old and studied the teachings of the Tendai sect. This sect was introduced to Japan by two

Japanese priests, Dengyō Daishi (767-822), who was in China in 804-5, and his pupil Jikaku Daishi (794-864), who was in China in 835-47. Enryakuji at Hieizan is the head temple of the sect. The teachings of Tendai are of very broad scope, and with a wealth of old Chinese publications and manuscripts in its libraries, Enryakuji was the center of learning for all Buddhist students. It seems that some priests, after years of study, found themselves with the conviction that religion is not philosophy. The scholar Eshin Sōzu advocated the importance of simple faith. Another Tendai priest, Kūya (896-972), spent the greater part of his life traveling and preaching a simple faith to the masses. He helped people of rural districts with their communal needs by building roads and improving water supplies. Ippen followed the steps of Kūya and traveled all over Japan from 1273 until his death. He founded the sect called Jishū which is closely related to the Jōdo sect. His enormous number of followers made possible the production of 11 hand scrolls illustrating his life and works. The work painted by En-i in 12 rolls is the finest, but there are at least three others in the list of national treasures.

In 1298, a year prior to the work by En-i, another noted hand scroll was painted by the Buddhist painter Rengyō. This work called "Tōsei Den," in five rolls, illustrates the life of the Chinese priest Chien-chen (Jap. Ganjin) (688 763), who came to Japan in 753 and founded the temple Tōshō-daiji. An account of the zeal and sacrifices of Ganjin and two Japanese priests, Eiei and Fushō, who spent 15 years in China from 733 to 748 in their efforts to have the Chinese leader come to Japan, reveal one of the most inspiring accounts in the history of Buddhism.

REFERENCE NOTES

The illustrations, however, consist mainly of Chinese scenes, and in the quality of painting, En-i is decidedly superior to Rengyō. Thus we may consider the work of "Ippen," painted in 1299, as the monumental scroll that established the form and characteristics of Japanese illustrated lives of the Buddhist priests.

The next large group of hand scrolls is on the life and works of the priest Hōnen (1131-1211), the founder of the Jōdo sect. These include seven works, totaling 82 rolls, headed by the famous 48 rolls of Chion-in which were painted in the early fourteenth century.

Another group of scrolls on the priest Ryōnin (1072-1132), called "Yūzū-nenbutsu Engi," requires special attention because of its printed reproduction. These scrolls were first painted in 1384, and again in 1390, and it is from the latter work, in two rolls each measuring 11 inches high and about 50 feet long, that block prints were reproduced. The work of engraving wooden blocks and printing was started in 1390 and finished in 1414.

A note given on the scroll states that the purpose of publication was to distribute one to each of the more than 60 provinces all over Japan, but it is not clear how many were actually made. Only two complete hand-colored printed rolls are extant, and these are kept at the temple Dai-Nenbutsuji, Osaka.

Many printed pictures of Buddhist images were made in Japan in the thirteenth century. We find some of them dated 1228, 1242, and 1256. A printed portrait of Hōnen, measuring 33 inches vertically with the date 1315, is kept at Chion-in.

The large scale and variety of subject matter represented

make the scenes in the printed scroll of "Yūzū-nenbutsu" a monument in the history of printed pictures in Japan. This work was a forerunner to the great number of illustrated books published after the early seventeenth century, which in turn lead to the later development of *ukiyo-e* prints. The enormous amount of time required for the production of the printed rolls seems to indicate, however, that the art of engraving printing blocks was in practice only for special cases in the late fourteenth and early fifteenth centuries.

All of these hand scrolls mentioned above illustrating the lives of Buddhist priests show a common characteristic: equal importance is given to the pictures of aristocrats and common people.

The financial support that enabled the production of these works came from all sources: the imperial court as well as poor rural communities, but in the hundreds of scenes that are shown in these rolls, not a single instance is found in which a donor is represented in the picture. These illustrations of the lives and works of Japanese priests seem to suggest that economic and social circumstances may not be the only factors that motivate human activities in art and religion.

Plates 20-21

Since the school is commonly known by the name of the artist Kōrin, we have followed it for the convenience of identification, but the book *Koga Bikō,* a very comprehensive reference work on Japanese painting compiled by Asoka Sakisada (1800-1856), a descendant of the famous painter Kano Tsunenobu (1636-1713), identifies the school as the School of Kōetsu.

It seems to be correct to give the credit to Kōetsu because he was the pioneer who introduced this form of painting. Visitors to the residence of Kōetsu in a suburb of Kyoto may notice a stone monument erected there in May, 1930 by Kōetsu Kai, a society devoted to the study and preservation of the art of Kōetsu, in memory of Charles Lang Freer, the American patron of art who greatly admired the works and personality of this painter.

The works of Kōetsu and his friend Sōtatsu show clearly that they found inspirations in the screen and scroll paintings by old *Yamato-e* artists. Their technique and their favorite subject matter in painting can be traced to sources in Japanese classics.

The two pictures of plum trees in the scroll painting by Mitsunaga (Plate 12) are of special interest in connection with a study of this school. Similarity in form can be noted if one compares them with the paintings of plum trees usually associated with Kōrin.

For generations the family of Ogata served as dressmaker to the imperial household. Kōrin's father studied the art of calligraphy under Kōetsu, and Kōetsu's elder sister was the wife of Kōrin's great grandfather. This background undoubtedly helped Kōrin to fully develop his talent and ability, and with his extravagant taste he was able to popularize this characteristically Japanese form of painting to a remarkable degree.

Plate 32

This painting is selected primarily as an example of the Kano school, representing both Japanese (in the portrait) and Chinese (in the waterfall painting) characteristics. Two points of interest, aside from mere technical features, attract our attention.

In the first place, this is a rare case in which a portrait of an artist with his wife was painted by their son.

Kaihoku Yūshō (1533-1615) was born to a samurai family of high rank, serving the lord Asai Nagamasa (1545-1573) who tragically met his end in a battle with the famous war lord Oda Nobunaga (1534-1582). Yūshō entered Buddhist life in his youth and thus escaped the savage struggles between war lords of that time. There is no record of his training as a painter. His distinctly individual style suggests that he was self-taught, probably studying old Chinese works available to him at temples. Although Yūshō was already over sixty when he was introduced to Toyotomi Hideyoshi (1536-1598) as a painter, he painted his screen masterpieces mainly under the patronage of Hideyoshi.

It is considered that Yūshō left the Buddhist life and married in the latter part of his life. He was sixty-five when his only son Yūsetsu was born. Yūsetsu was seventeen when his father died, and he could not have fully mastered his painting technique even if he started training under his father very early in childhood. It seems more likely that he painted this portrait from memory, after he had established his position as an official painter to the shogun Tokugawa Iemitsu (1604-1651). His mother was probably still alive then and gave advice for this portrait.

Yūsetsu (1598-1677) did not follow his father's style in painting but became a painter of the Kano school, the official style of Tokugawa.

Secondly, the introduction of a painting of the Chinese poet Li Po at a waterfall has special significance. In the collection of literary works by the Zen priest Genso (1537-1611), noted for his poetry in Chinese form, he remarks on a painting by Yūshō of Li Po at a waterfall and includes in the note a poem about the painting. Apparently the painting had a special quality and might have been one of the artist's favorite works. Still mounted on board in this portrait, the painting shows it being examined after the work was done. A scene of his father and mother inspecting his painting with satisfaction should be just what a son would be most eager to keep.

Plates 34, 35, 36

Contemporary with Ōkyo and equally noted as a naturalistic painter who based his study on old Chinese works, Itō Jakuchū (1716-1800) should be remembered as one of the distinguished masters in the history of Japanese painting.

Jakuchū was the proprietor of a green-grocery in Kyoto and started his career as a painter early in life, as his talent was recognized in childhood. His first training was under a Kano painter, but he developed his own style by studying old Chinese works and the works of Kōrin. He was versatile in his technique and could paint equally well in the bold abstraction of brush strokes and the naturalistic representation of minut colore delineation.

It is said that he occasionally displayed some paintings at his store, with price tags in an amount of rice, and as soon as he obtained half a bushel of rice by the sale of his pictures, he closed his store for the day.

Jakuchū was interested in Zen Buddhism and spent the latter part of his life in seclusion as a Zen Buddhist. When he finished his 30 famous paintings depicting naturalistic subjects, he decided to present them to the temple Shō-kokuji in Kyoto, as he evidently valued these works so much that he sought a permanent home for them. These 30 paintings on *kakemono* were later transferred to the Imperial Collection.

Jakuchū's drawings, published in an album printed in white on black, show the artist's characteristics. Drawings represent flowering plants, fruit, and insects, with all plant and insect forms faithfully delineated, yet the pictures are organized into beautiful designs.

Compared to the romantic Kōrin, Jakuchū is decidedly a realist. He carried his study of nature to a point very few Japanese painters had been able to reach. It is remarkable that despite his minute care for details he still kept his designs clear and forceful. Jakuchū was an independent artist and had no followers to succeed him.

APPENDICES

Japanese Art Today

All phases of painting in present day Japan are a continuation of what has been done in past centuries. One may notice traces of the schools of Buddhist, *Yamato-e,* Kano, Ōkyo, Chinese literati, or the naturalists still persisting to some extent in the great number of works produced in every conceivable form. The majority of contemporary Japanese painters, of course, are eclectics.

Especially with the prevailing influence of Western culture in our time, artists can no longer keep themselves aloof from the international complex. Foreign influence has always been an essential part of Japanese culture, and to the grace and refinement of racial characteristics which tend to become too delicate, Continental influences gave depth and strength. Relief from stagnation, inevitable in insular isolation, was constantly sought from abroad.

As a part of Oriental culture, Japanese art holds its own in accomplishment, besides being the intermediary that links the ancient traditions of China and India to the arts of the modern world.

Chronological Table

Japanese Painters in Chronological Order

Most of the masterpieces of Japanese Buddhist paintings bear neither inscriptions concerning the artists nor dates, and we have no adequate records about the circumstances in which those works were done. In the biographies of old *Yamato-e* painters, however, we find many accounts of their Buddhist works.

Almost all of the court painters in the Heian period, including their first master, Kanaoka, and his descendants, are credited with excellence in Buddhist painting. There was a close relation between the imperial court and the temples, and the artists did not limit their subject matter.

One could probably assume that a number of great works attributed to the priests like Kōbō Daishi or Chishō Daishi were done by some of the Yamato-e painters.

Yamato-e
  Kose no Kanaoka (active 859-900)
  Fujiwara Takayoshi (active around 1110)
  Toba Sōjō (1053-1140)
  Fujiwara Mitsunaga (active around 1173)
  Tosa Tsunetaka (active around 1170)
  Sumiyoshi Keion (active around 1200)
  Fujiwara Takanobu (1142-1205)

Fujiwara Nobuzane (1177-1265)
Tosa Yoshimitsu (active around 1300)
Takashina Takakane (active around 1309)

Buddhist
Eshin Sōzu (942-1017)
Takuma Tamenari (active around 1050)
Takuma Shōga (active around 1200)
Minchō (2012-91)

Ukiyo-e
Hishikawa Moronobu (1618-95)
Torii Kiyonobu (1664-1729)
Nishikawa Sukenobu (active 1671-1751)
Okamura Masanobu (1685-1764)
Suzuki Harunobu (1725-70)
Katsukawa Shunshō (1726-92)
Kitagawa Utamaro (1733-1806)
Kitao Shigemasa (1740-1819)
Torii Kiyonaga (1752-1815)
Katsushika Hokusai (1760-1849)
Utagawa Toyokuni (1768-1825)
Andō Hiroshige (1797-1858)

School of Kōrin
Honnami Kōetsu (1557-1637)
Tawaraya Sōtatsu (?-1643)
Ogata Kōrin (1655-1716)
Sakai Hōitsu (1761-1828)

Chinese Schools and the Eclectics

Kaō (?-1345)
Shūbun (active around 1450)
Shukō (1420-1502)
Sesshū (1420-1506)
Kano Motonobu (1476-1559)
Kaihoku Yūshō (1533-1615)
Hasegawa Tōhaku (1539-1610)
Kano Eitoku (1543-90)
Kano Sanraku (1559-1635)
Gion Nankai (1677-1751)
Itō Jakuchū (1716-1800)
Ikeno Taigadō (1723-76)
Yosa Buson (1724-83)
Maruyama Ōkyo (1733-95)
Matsumura Goshun (1752-1811)
Tani Bunchō (1763-1840)
Okamoto Shūki (1785-1862)
Watanabe Kazan (1793-1841)

The Mon-yo *or crests reproduced throughout this book are family designs used on clothing and personal possessions. The history of the* Mon-yo *dates back to 4,000 B. C. and even to-day Japanese descendants utilise these family motifs.*

Illustrated on the title page is the author's family crest.